ALLIE SKYE FLIES

A

Copyright © 2023 Allie Skye Ltd.

All rights reserved.

No part of this book may be reproduced or transmitted in any form or by any means, electronic or mechanical, including photocopying, recording, or by any information storage and retrieval system, without written permission from the author.

A CIP catalogue record of this book is available from the British Library.

ISBN: 978-1-7392389-1-9
Printed in United Kingdom

2 4 6 8 10 9 7 5 3 1

www.allieskye.com

For Great Auntie Katie

&

For Great Auntie Gladys, who was always up for an adventure

One bright morning in Australia, Allie Skye was woken up by her mummy and daddy to begin an amazing adventure. Allie Skye and Daddy would be getting a little aeroplane and then a big aeroplane to fly to Scotland to meet Nanny Scotland.

Mummy took Allie Skye and Daddy to the airport. Nonna Farm met them there as she wanted to wave them off on their big trip!

Allie Skye was so excited to jump onto the little aeroplane that she forgot to say goodbye to Nonna Farm. As the plane took off, Allie Skye held her stuffed kangaroo up to the window. "Wombat, say goodbye to all the kookaburras and snakes below," she said.

The little plane soon landed, and Allie Skye and Daddy found the check-in desk. Behind the counter was a lady with a big, kind smile. She reminded Allie Skye a lot of her mummy at home. "Hello, Allie Skye. My name's Jacinta and I'll be helping you board your flight," she said.

Allie Skye showed her passport and one that she had made for Wombat.

Next, Jacinta weighed her luggage and then weighed Wombat too. In case he had excess luggage in his pouch!

The next stop was security. Allie Skye watched her bag go through the X-ray machine. She spotted her Vegemite and boomerang.

Next, it was Wombat's turn.

Daddy helped Allie Skye to fill in a declaration card for Nonna's special sauce and they passed through to the gate to wait to board the big plane.

Allie Skye felt scared looking at the big plane, so Daddy called Nonna Farm on his tablet. "I forgot to say goodbye to you," said Allie Skye, feeling sad.

"My love," said Nonna Farm. "It is never goodbye. Every night, we can both look at the same skies and stars. And, as sure as day becomes night, know that I'll be holding you tight in my heart."

Allie Skye's eyes were wide as they boarded the big plane. She had a seat all to herself, and one for Wombat too!

The air hostess gave Allie Skye a bag of goodies. Allie Skye was so busy colouring that she didn't even notice they were now flying ever so high, way up in the sky.

Before long, an air hostess arrived with Allie Skye and Daddy's dinner. It reminded Allie Skye of her kindie packed lunch box with special compartments full of delicious treats.

After dinner, the lights inside the plane dimmed, and Allie Skye began to feel sleepy. Daddy helped Allie Skye to get all snuggly. As Daddy pulled down the blind, Allie Skye looked out of the little window and spotted the brightest star in the sky.

"Night night, Nonna Farm. Night night, Nanny Scotland," she yawned. Then Allie Skye and Wombat gave themselves a virtual cuddle and drifted off to sleep.

Allie Skye woke up the next morning as Daddy opened the blind. Allie Skye had never seen the ocean before.

"Wow, Wombat! Look at the bright, blue sea!" she said, as the big aeroplane swooped down to land at Edinburgh Airport.

After landing, Allie Skye, Daddy, and Wombat walked through arrivals and got onto a tram. It took them to a railway station and, as the train pulled out, Allie Skye saw Edinburgh Castle.
Her first real-life castle ever!

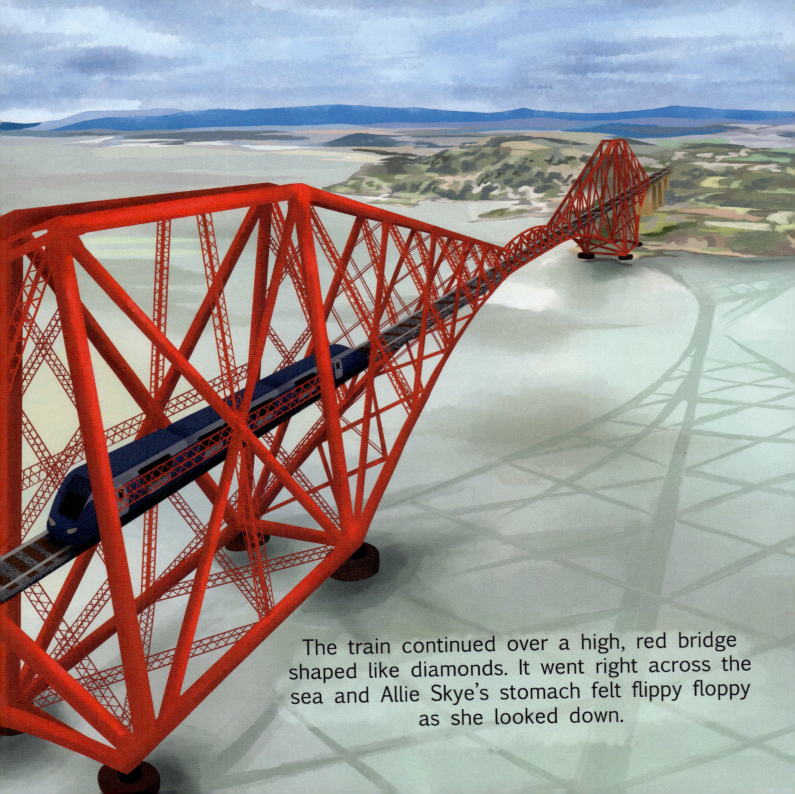

The train continued over a high, red bridge shaped like diamonds. It went right across the sea and Allie Skye's stomach felt flippy floppy as she looked down.

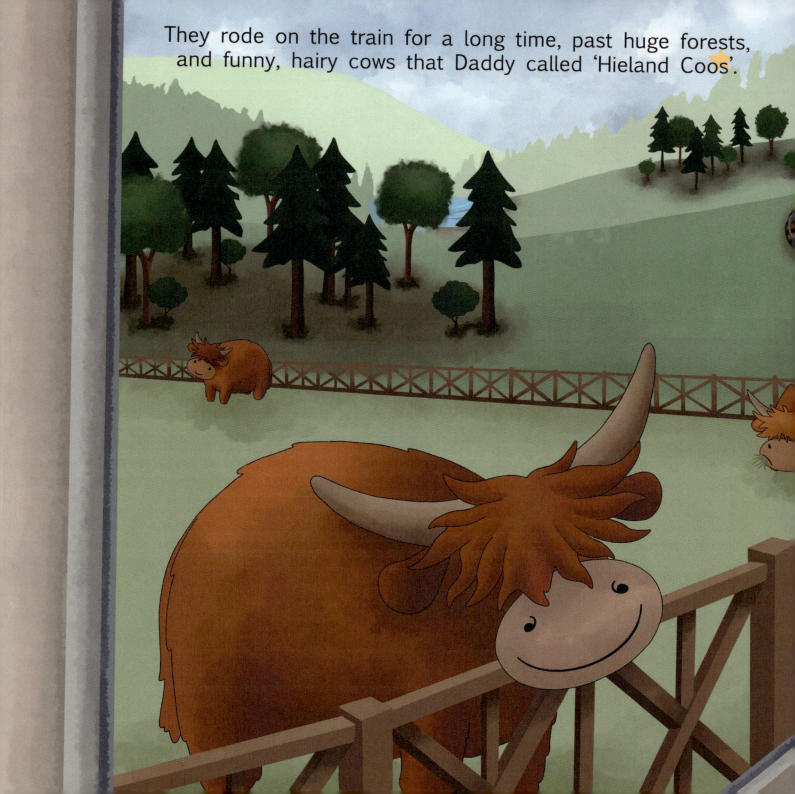
They rode on the train for a long time, past huge forests, and funny, hairy cows that Daddy called 'Hieland Coos'.

They travelled along the coast, around lochs that were so winding and wobbly that Allie Skye regretted eating so much shortbread from the train trolley!

Finally, the train began to slow and, as it pulled into the station, they could see Nanny Scotland waiting.

"My love, you've arrived. Oh, and Wombat's brought me my favourite. Nonna's special sauce!" she said, peeking into Wombat's pouch.

"Look, Wombat, I've brought you a present too," said Nanny Scotland. "Meet Nessie."

Daddy put the luggage into Nanny Scotland's car, and they all got in. And, with Wombat holding one of Allie Skye's hands, and Nessie the other, they drove onto the bridge that goes over the sea to Skye.

Allie Skye's Guide

- **Nanny Scotland** – My daddy's mummy. She lives on an island called Skye.
- **Nonna Farm** – My mummy's mummy. Her mummy came to Australia from Italy.
- **Kangaroo** – An animal which only lives in Australia. It stands on its back legs and jumps all bouncy.
- **Wombat** – My cuddly toy Kangaroo. I named him after a small, furry animal from Australia.
- **Kookaburra** – I think this is the prettiest songbird that lives in Australia.
- **Check-in desk** – Where you go to say hello and get a ticket for the plane.
- **Passport** – A mini book with your name and picture in. You show this to get your ticket.
- **Excess luggage** – If you take too many bags to go on the plane.
- **Security** – A check to make sure your luggage is safe to go on the plane.
- **X-ray machine** – It lets you see inside the luggage without opening it.
- **Vegemite** – I like to put this on my toast for breakfast.
- **Boomerang** – Long ago in Australia it was used for hunting, but now we use it like a Frisbee.
- **Declaration card** – Daddy says you must fill this in to take certain foods to Scotland.
- **Nonna's special sauce** – It's so special I can't tell you... what do you think is in it?

- ⭐ Gate – Where the aeroplanes park and wait for us.
- ⭐ Tablet – A screen you can use to talk or play games on.
- ⭐ Air hostess – A person who works on the plane and helps keep you safe.
- ⭐ Kindie – Kindergarten. When I complete this, I will go to big school.
- ⭐ Virtual cuddle – When someone can't be with you, you hold yourself tight and pretend it is them.
- ⭐ Edinburgh – Daddy says this is the capital of Scotland.
- ⭐ Arrivals – You walk through here to exit the airport.
- ⭐ Tram – It is like a train, but it is electric and runs beside cars on the road.
- ⭐ Edinburgh Castle – Where kings and queens used to live.
- ⭐ Hieland Coo – Highland cow. These are big, red, and hairy. Just like Daddy!
- ⭐ Loch – What a lake is called in Scotland.
- ⭐ Shortbread – A yummy, crumbly biscuit made in Scotland.
- ⭐ Train trolley – It serves you snacks and hot and cold drinks on long train journeys.
- ⭐ Nessie – This is a big, green water beastie that lives in Scotland but is very shy.
- ⭐ Skye – Where Daddy grew up and where all my Scottish family live.

Now, let's go and meet them!

Visit allieskye.com to download free Allie Skye printables and to join our mailing list for news on future books, activities, competitions and more.

By the author

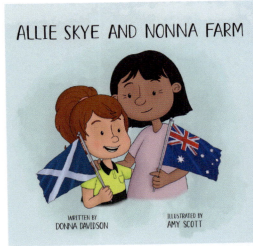
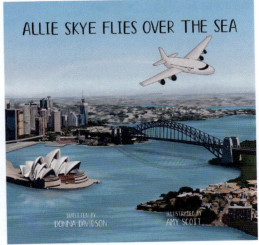
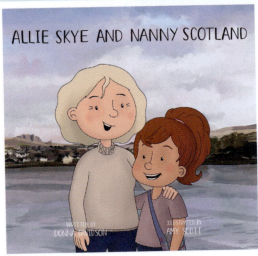

Buy now by visiting www.allieskye.com

About the Author

Donna Davidson was raised on the Isle of Skye, enjoying a magnificent view from her childhood home looking across the bay of Portree. Donna studied creative writing before travelling to Australia, where she lived and worked for two years before returning to Scotland and settling in the Kingdom of Fife with her cat, Vlad. She has two older brothers. Paul, her eldest brother, has recently returned to live in Portree with his wife, Jemma. Meanwhile, Grant lives in Griffith, New South Wales, Australia with his wife, Jacinta, and their four children: Chloe Skye, Allie, Holly, and Angus.

Inspired by her nieces and nephew, and strengthening their connection with Scotland, Donna returned to her passion for writing.

Thus, the Allie Skye series of books was created. You can contact Allie Skye or Donna by emailing hello@allieskye.com.

About the Illustrator

Amy Scott was born in Edinburgh, Scotland, going on to study Animation at The University of Edinburgh. You can find more illustration and portrait work at amyscottart.co.uk.

Printed in Great Britain
by Amazon